CONTENTS

CHAPTER FOUR
GOD PREPARES A CITY FOR THEM
(cf. *Heb* 11:16)

1. THE LIGHT OF FAITH: this is how the Church's tradition speaks of the great gift brought by Jesus. In John's Gospel, Christ says of himself: "I have come as light into the world, that whoever believes in me may not remain in darkness" (*Jn* 12:46). Saint Paul uses the same image: "God who said 'Let light shine out of darkness,' has shone in our hearts" (*2 Cor* 4:6). The pagan world, which hungered for light, had seen the growth of the cult of the sun god, *Sol Invictus*, invoked each day at sunrise. Yet though the sun was born anew each morning, it was clearly incapable of casting its light on all of human existence. The sun does not illumine all reality; its rays cannot penetrate to the shadow of death, the place where men's eyes are closed to its light. "No one — Saint Justin Martyr writes — has ever been ready to die for his faith in the sun".[1] Conscious of the immense horizon which their faith opened before them, Christians invoked Jesus as the true sun "whose rays bestow life".[2] To Martha, weeping for the death of her brother Lazarus, Jesus said: "Did I not tell you that if you believed, you would see the glory of God?" (*Jn* 11:40). Those who believe, see; they see with a light that illumines their

[1] *Dialogus cum Tryphone Iudaeo*, 121, 2: PG 6, 758.
[2] CLEMENT OF ALEXANDRIA, *Protrepticus*, IX: PG 8, 195.

entire journey, for it comes from the risen Christ, the morning star which never sets.

An illusory light?

2. Yet in speaking of the light of faith, we can almost hear the objections of many of our contemporaries. In modernity, that light might have been considered sufficient for societies of old, but was felt to be of no use for new times, for a humanity come of age, proud of its rationality and anxious to explore the future in novel ways. Faith thus appeared to some as an illusory light, preventing mankind from boldly setting out in quest of knowledge. The young Nietzsche encouraged his sister Elisabeth to take risks, to tread "new paths... with all the uncertainty of one who must find his own way", adding that "this is where humanity's paths part: if you want peace of soul and happiness, then believe, but if you want to be a follower of truth, then seek".[3] Belief would be incompatible with seeking. From this starting point Nietzsche was to develop his critique of Christianity for diminishing the full meaning of human existence and stripping life of novelty and adventure. Faith would thus be the illusion of light, an illusion which blocks the path of a liberated humanity to its future.

3. In the process, faith came to be associated with darkness. There were those who tried to save

[3] *Brief an Elisabeth Nietzsche* (11 June 1865), in: *Werke in drei Bänden*, München, 1954, 953ff.

4

faith by making room for it alongside the light of reason. Such room would open up wherever the light of reason could not penetrate, wherever certainty was no longer possible. Faith was thus understood either as a leap in the dark, to be taken in the absence of light, driven by blind emotion, or as a subjective light, capable perhaps of warming the heart and bringing personal consolation, but not something which could be proposed to others as an objective and shared light which points the way. Slowly but surely, however, it would become evident that the light of autonomous reason is not enough to illumine the future; ultimately the future remains shadowy and fraught with fear of the unknown. As a result, humanity renounced the search for a great light, Truth itself, in order to be content with smaller lights which illumine the fleeting moment yet prove incapable of showing the way. Yet in the absence of light everything becomes confused; it is impossible to tell good from evil, or the road to our destination from other roads which take us in endless circles, going nowhere.

A light to be recovered

4.   There is an urgent need, then, to see once again that faith is a light, for once the flame of faith dies out, all other lights begin to dim. The light of faith is unique, since it is capable of illuminating *every aspect* of human existence. For a light to be this powerful it cannot come from ourselves; it must come from a more primordial

source: in a word, it must come from God. Faith is born of an encounter with the living God who calls us and reveals his love, a love which precedes us and upon which we can lean for security and for building our lives. Transformed by this love, we gain fresh vision, new eyes to see; we realize that it contains a great promise of fulfilment, and that a vision of the future opens up before us. Faith, received from God as a supernatural gift, becomes a light for our way, guiding our journey through time. On the one hand, it is a light coming from the past, the light of the foundational memory of the life of Jesus which revealed his perfectly trustworthy love, a love capable of triumphing over death. Yet since Christ has risen and draws us beyond death, faith is also a light coming from the future and opening before us vast horizons which guide us beyond our isolated selves towards the breadth of communion. We come to see that faith does not dwell in shadow and gloom; it is a light for our darkness. Dante, in the Divine Comedy, after professing his faith to Saint Peter, describes that light as a "spark, which then becomes a burning flame and like a heavenly star within me glimmers".[4] It is this light of faith that I would now like to consider, so that it can grow and enlighten the present, becoming a star to brighten the horizon of our journey at a time when mankind is particularly in need of light.

---

[4] Paradiso XXIV, 145-147.

5.   Christ, on the eve of his passion, assured Peter: "I have prayed for you that your faith may not fail" (*Lk* 22:32). He then told him to strengthen his brothers and sisters in that same faith. Conscious of the duty entrusted to the Successor of Peter, Benedict XVI proclaimed the present Year of Faith, a time of grace which is helping us to sense the great joy of believing and to renew our wonder at the vast horizons which faith opens up, so as then to profess that faith in its unity and integrity, faithful to the memory of the Lord and sustained by his presence and by the working of the Holy Spirit. The conviction born of a faith which brings grandeur and fulfilment to life, a faith centred on Christ and on the power of his grace, inspired the mission of the first Christians. In the acts of the martyrs, we read the following dialogue between the Roman prefect Rusticus and a Christian named Hierax: "'Where are your parents?', the judge asked the martyr. He replied: 'Our true father is Christ, and our mother is faith in him'".[5] For those early Christians, faith, as an encounter with the living God revealed in Christ, was indeed a "mother", for it had brought them to the light and given birth within them to divine life, a new experience and a luminous vision of existence for which they were prepared to bear public witness to the end.

6.   The Year of Faith was inaugurated on the fiftieth anniversary of the opening of the Second

---

[5] *Acta Sanctorum*, Junii, I, 21.

Vatican Council. This is itself a clear indication that Vatican II was a Council on faith,[6] inasmuch as it asked us to restore the primacy of God in Christ to the centre of our lives, both as a Church and as individuals. The Church never takes faith for granted, but knows that this gift of God needs to be nourished and reinforced so that it can continue to guide her pilgrim way. The Second Vatican Council enabled the light of faith to illumine our human experience from within, accompanying the men and women of our time on their journey. It clearly showed how faith enriches life in all its dimensions.

7. These considerations on faith — in continuity with all that the Church's magisterium has pronounced on this theological virtue[7] — are meant to supplement what Benedict XVI had written in his encyclical letters on charity and hope. He himself had almost completed a first draft of an encyclical on faith. For this I am deeply grateful

---

[6] "Though the Council does not expressly deal with faith, it speaks of it on every page, it recognizes its living, supernatural character, it presumes it to be full and strong, and it bases its teachings on it. It is sufficient to recall the Council's statements... to see the essential importance which the Council, in line with the doctrinal tradition of the Church, attributes to faith, the true faith, which has its source in Christ, and the magisterium of the Church for its channel" (Paul VI, General Audience [8 March 1967]: *Insegnamenti* V [1967], 705).

[7] Cf., for example, FIRST VATICAN ECUMENICAL COUNCIL, Dogmatic Constitution on the Catholic Faith *Dei Filius*, Ch. 3: DS 3008-3020; SECOND VATICAN ECUMENICAL COUNCIL, Dogmatic Constitution on Divine Revelation *Dei Verbum*, 5: *Cate- chism of the Catholic Church*, Nos. 153-165.

to him, and as his brother in Christ I have taken up his fine work and added a few contributions of my own. The Successor of Peter, yesterday, today and tomorrow, is always called to strengthen his brothers and sisters in the priceless treasure of that faith which God has given as a light for humanity's path.

In God's gift of faith, a supernatural infused virtue, we realize that a great love has been offered us, a good word has been spoken to us, and that when we welcome that word, Jesus Christ the Word made flesh, the Holy Spirit transforms us, lights up our way to the future and enables us joyfully to advance along that way on wings of hope. Thus wonderfully interwoven, faith, hope and charity are the driving force of the Christian life as it advances towards full communion with God. But what is it like, this road which faith opens up before us? What is the origin of this powerful light which brightens the journey of a successful and fruitful life?

CHAPTER ONE

WE HAVE BELIEVED IN LOVE
(cf. *1 Jn* 4:16)

Abraham, our father in faith

8.   Faith opens the way before us and accompanies our steps through time. Hence, if we want to understand what faith is, we need to follow the route it has taken, the path trodden by believers, as witnessed first in the Old Testament. Here a unique place belongs to Abraham, our father in faith. Something disturbing takes place in his life: God speaks to him; he reveals himself as a God who speaks and calls his name. Faith is linked to hearing. Abraham does not see God, but hears his voice. Faith thus takes on a personal aspect. God is not the god of a particular place, or a deity linked to specific sacred time, but the God of a person, the God of Abraham, Isaac and Jacob, capable of interacting with man and establishing a covenant with him. Faith is our response to a word which engages us personally, to a "Thou" who calls us by name.

9.   The word spoken to Abraham contains both a call and a promise. First, it is a call to leave his own land, a summons to a new life, the beginning of an exodus which points him towards an unforeseen future. The sight which faith would give to Abraham would always be linked to the need to take this step forward: faith "sees" to the

extent that it journeys, to the extent that it chooses to enter into the horizons opened up by God's word. This word also contains a promise: Your descendants will be great in number, you will be the father of a great nation (cf. *Gen* 13:16; 15:5; 22:17). As a response to a word which preceded it, Abraham's faith would always be an act of remembrance. Yet this remembrance is not fixed on past events but, as the memory of a promise, it becomes capable of opening up the future, shedding light on the path to be taken. We see how faith, as remembrance of the future, *memoria futuri*, is thus closely bound up with hope.

10.   Abraham is asked to entrust himself to this word. Faith understands that something so apparently ephemeral and fleeting as a word, when spoken by the God who is fidelity, becomes absolutely certain and unshakable, guaranteeing the continuity of our journey through history. Faith accepts this word as a solid rock upon which we can build, a straight highway on which we can travel. In the Bible, faith is expressed by the Hebrew word *'emûnāh*, derived from the verb *'amān* whose root means "to uphold". The term *'emûnāh* can signify both God's fidelity and man's faith. The man of faith gains strength by putting himself in the hands of the God who is faithful. Playing on this double meaning of the word — also found in the corresponding terms in Greek (*pistós*) and Latin (*fidelis*) — Saint Cyril of Jerusalem praised the dignity of the Christian

who receives God's own name: both are called "faithful".[8] As Saint Augustine explains: "Man is faithful when he believes in God and his promises; God is faithful when he grants to man what he has promised".[9]

11.   A final element of the story of Abraham is important for understanding his faith. God's word, while bringing newness and surprise, is not at all alien to Abraham's experience. In the voice which speaks to him, the patriarch recognizes a profound call which was always present at the core of his being. God ties his promise to that aspect of human life which has always appeared most "full of promise", namely, parenthood, the begetting of new life: "Sarah your wife shall bear you a son, and you shall name him Isaac" (*Gen* 17:19). The God who asks Abraham for complete trust reveals himself to be the source of all life. Faith is thus linked to God's fatherhood, which gives rise to all creation; the God who calls Abraham is the Creator, the one who "calls into existence the things that do not exist" (*Rom* 4:17), the one who "chose us before the foundation of the world... and destined us for adoption as his children" (*Eph* 1:4-5). For Abraham, faith in God sheds light on the depths of his being, it enables him to acknowledge the wellspring of goodness at the origin of all things and to realize that his life is not the product of

---

[8]   Cf. *Catechesis* V, 1: PG 33, 505A.
[9]   *In Psal.* 32, II, s. I, 9: PL 36, 284.

non-being or chance, but the fruit of a personal call and a personal love. The mysterious God who called him is no alien deity, but the God who is the origin and mainstay of all that is. The great test of Abraham's faith, the sacrifice of his son Isaac, would show the extent to which this primordial love is capable of ensuring life even beyond death. The word which could raise up a son to one who was "as good as dead", in "the barrenness" of Sarah's womb (cf. *Rom* 4:19), can also stand by his promise of a future beyond all threat or danger (cf. *Heb* 11:19; *Rom* 4:21).

The faith of Israel

12.   The history of the people of Israel in the Book of Exodus follows in the wake of Abraham's faith. Faith once again is born of a primordial gift: Israel trusts in God, who promises to set his people free from their misery. Faith becomes a summons to a lengthy journey leading to worship of the Lord on Sinai and the inheritance of a promised land. God's love is seen to be like that of a father who carries his child along the way (cf. *Dt* 1:31). Israel's confession of faith takes shape as an account of God's deeds in setting his people free and acting as their guide (cf. *Dt* 26:5-11), an account passed down from one generation to the next. God's light shines for Israel through the remembrance of the Lord's mighty deeds, recalled and celebrated in worship, and passed down from parents to children. Here we see how the light of faith is linked to con-

crete life-stories, to the grateful remembrance of God's mighty deeds and the progressive fulfilment of his promises. Gothic architecture gave clear expression to this: in the great cathedrals light comes down from heaven by passing through windows depicting the history of salvation. God's light comes to us through the account of his self-revelation, and thus becomes capable of illuminating our passage through time by recalling his gifts and demonstrating how he fulfils his promises.

13. The history of Israel also shows us the temptation of unbelief to which the people yielded more than once. Here the opposite of faith is shown to be idolatry. While Moses is speaking to God on Sinai, the people cannot bear the mystery of God's hiddenness, they cannot endure the time of waiting to see his face. Faith by its very nature demands renouncing the immediate possession which sight would appear to offer; it is an invitation to turn to the source of the light, while respecting the mystery of a countenance which will unveil itself personally in its own good time. Martin Buber once cited a definition of idolatry proposed by the rabbi of Kock: idolatry is "when a face addresses a face which is not a face".[10] In place of faith in God, it seems better to worship an idol, into whose face we can look directly and whose origin we

---

[10] M. BUBER, *Die Erzählungen der Chassidim*, Zürich, 1949, 793.

know, because it is the work of our own hands. Before an idol, there is no risk that we will be called to abandon our security, for idols "have mouths, but they cannot speak" (*Ps* 115:5). Idols exist, we begin to see, as a pretext for setting ourselves at the centre of reality and worshiping the work of our own hands. Once man has lost the fundamental orientation which unifies his existence, he breaks down into the multiplicity of his desires; in refusing to await the time of promise, his life-story disintegrates into a myriad of unconnected instants. Idolatry, then, is always polytheism, an aimless passing from one lord to another. Idolatry does not offer a journey but rather a plethora of paths leading nowhere and forming a vast labyrinth. Those who choose not to put their trust in God must hear the din of countless idols crying out: "Put your trust in me!" Faith, tied as it is to conversion, is the opposite of idolatry; it breaks with idols to turn to the living God in a personal encounter. Believing means entrusting oneself to a merciful love which always accepts and pardons, which sustains and directs our lives, and which shows its power by its ability to make straight the crooked lines of our history. Faith consists in the willingness to let ourselves be constantly transformed and renewed by God's call. Herein lies the paradox: by constantly turning towards the Lord, we discover a sure path which liberates us from the dissolution imposed upon us by idols.

14.   In the faith of Israel we also encounter the figure of Moses, the mediator. The people may not see the face of God; it is Moses who speaks to YHWH on the mountain and then tells the others of the Lord's will. With this presence of a mediator in its midst, Israel learns to journey together in unity. The individual's act of faith finds its place within a community, within the common "we" of the people who, in faith, are like a single person — "my first-born son", as God would describe all of Israel (cf. *Ex* 4:22). Here mediation is not an obstacle, but an opening: through our encounter with others, our gaze rises to a truth greater than ourselves. Rousseau once lamented that he could not see God for himself: "How many people stand between God and me!"[11] … "Is it really so simple and natural that God would have sought out Moses in order to speak to Jean Jacques Rousseau?"[12] On the basis of an individualistic and narrow conception of knowledge one cannot appreciate the significance of mediation, this capacity to participate in the vision of another, this shared knowledge which is the knowledge proper to love. Faith is God's free gift, which calls for humility and the courage to trust and to entrust; it enables us to see the luminous path leading to the encounter of God and humanity: the history of salvation.

[11]   *Émile*, Paris, 1966, 387.
[12]   *Lettre à Christophe de Beaumont*, Lausanne, 1993, 110.

15. "Abraham rejoiced that he would see my day; he saw it and was glad" (*Jn* 8:56). According to these words of Jesus, Abraham's faith pointed to him; in some sense it foresaw his mystery. So Saint Augustine understood it when he stated that the patriarchs were saved by faith, not faith in Christ who had come but in Christ who was yet to come, a faith pressing towards the future of Jesus.[13] Christian faith is centred on Christ; it is the confession that Jesus is Lord and that God has raised him from the dead (cf. *Rom* 10:9). All the threads of the Old Testament converge on Christ; he becomes the definitive "Yes" to all the promises, the ultimate basis of our "Amen" to God (cf. *2 Cor* 1:20). The history of Jesus is the complete manifestation of God's reliability. If Israel continued to recall God's great acts of love, which formed the core of its confession of faith and broadened its gaze in faith, the life of Jesus now appears as the locus of God's definitive intervention, the supreme manifestation of his love for us. The word which God speaks to us in Jesus is not simply one word among many, but his eternal Word (cf. *Heb* 1:1-2). God can give no greater guarantee of his love, as Saint Paul reminds us (cf. *Rom* 8:31-39). Christian faith is thus faith in a perfect love, in its decisive power, in its ability to transform the world and to unfold its history. "We know and believe the love that

---

[13] Cf. *In Ioh. Evang.*, 45, 9: PL 35, 1722-1723.

God has for us" (*1 Jn* 4:16). In the love of God revealed in Jesus, faith perceives the foundation on which all reality and its final destiny rest.

16.	The clearest proof of the reliability of Christ's love is to be found in his dying for our sake. If laying down one's life for one's friends is the greatest proof of love (cf. *Jn* 15:13), Jesus offered his own life for all, even for his enemies, to transform their hearts. This explains why the evangelists could see the hour of Christ's crucifixion as the culmination of the gaze of faith; in that hour the depth and breadth of God's love shone forth. It was then that Saint John offered his solemn testimony, as together with the Mother of Jesus he gazed upon the pierced one (cf. *Jn* 19:37): "He who saw this has borne witness, so that you also may believe. His testimony is true, and he knows that he tells the truth" (*Jn* 19:35). In Dostoevsky's *The Idiot*, Prince Myshkin sees a painting by Hans Holbein the Younger depicting Christ dead in the tomb and says: "Looking at that painting might cause one to lose his faith".[14] The painting is a gruesome portrayal of the destructive effects of death on Christ's body. Yet it is precisely in contemplating Jesus' death that faith grows stronger and receives a dazzling light; then it is revealed as faith in Christ's steadfast love for us, a love capable of embracing death to bring us salvation. This love, which did not

---

[14]	Part II, IV.

recoil before death in order to show its depth, is something I can believe in; Christ's total self-gift overcomes every suspicion and enables me to entrust myself to him completely.

17.   Christ's death discloses the utter reliability of God's love above all in the light of his resurrection. As the risen one, Christ is the trustworthy witness, deserving of faith (cf. *Rev* 1:5; *Heb* 2:17), and a solid support for our faith. "If Christ has not been raised, your faith is futile", says Saint Paul (*1 Cor* 15:17). Had the Father's love not caused Jesus to rise from the dead, had it not been able to restore his body to life, then it would not be a completely reliable love, capable of illuminating also the gloom of death. When Saint Paul describes his new life in Christ, he speaks of "faith in the Son of God, who loved me and gave himself for me" (*Gal* 2:20). Clearly, this "faith in the Son of God" means Paul's faith in Jesus, but it also presumes that Jesus himself is worthy of faith, based not only on his having loved us even unto death but also on his divine sonship. Precisely because Jesus is the Son, because he is absolutely grounded in the Father, he was able to conquer death and make the fullness of life shine forth. Our culture has lost its sense of God's tangible presence and activity in our world. We think that God is to be found in the beyond, on another level of reality, far removed from our everyday relationships. But if this were the case, if God could not act in the world, his love would not

be truly powerful, truly real, and thus not even true, a love capable of delivering the bliss that it promises. It would make no difference at all whether we believed in him or not. Christians, on the contrary, profess their faith in God's tangible and powerful love which really does act in history and determines its final destiny: a love that can be encountered, a love fully revealed in Christ's passion, death and resurrection.

18. This fullness which Jesus brings to faith has another decisive aspect. In faith, Christ is not simply the one in whom we believe, the supreme manifestation of God's love; he is also the one with whom we are united precisely in order to believe. Faith does not merely gaze at Jesus, but sees things as Jesus himself sees them, with his own eyes: it is a participation in his way of seeing. In many areas in our lives we trust others who know more than we do. We trust the architect who builds our home, the pharmacist who gives us medicine for healing, the lawyer who defends us in court. We also need someone trustworthy and knowledgeable where God is concerned. Jesus, the Son of God, is the one who makes God known to us (cf. *Jn* 1:18). Christ's life, his way of knowing the Father and living in complete and constant relationship with him, opens up new and inviting vistas for human experience. Saint John brings out the importance of a personal relationship with Jesus for our faith by using various forms of the verb "to believe". In

addition to "believing that" what Jesus tells us is true, John also speaks of "believing" Jesus and "believing in" Jesus. We "believe" Jesus when we accept his word, his testimony, because he is truthful. We "believe in" Jesus when we personally welcome him into our lives and journey towards him, clinging to him in love and following in his footsteps along the way.

To enable us to know, accept and follow him, the Son of God took on our flesh. In this way he also saw the Father humanly, within the setting of a journey unfolding in time. Christian faith is faith in the incarnation of the Word and his bodily resurrection; it is faith in a God who is so close to us that he entered our human history. Far from divorcing us from reality, our faith in the Son of God made man in Jesus of Nazareth enables us to grasp reality's deepest meaning and to see how much God loves this world and is constantly guiding it towards himself. This leads us, as Christians, to live our lives in this world with ever greater commitment and intensity.

Salvation by faith

19. On the basis of this sharing in Jesus' way of seeing things, Saint Paul has left us a description of the life of faith. In accepting the gift of faith, believers become a new creation; they receive a new being; as God's children, they are now "sons in the Son". The phrase "Abba, Father", so characteristic of Jesus' own experience, now becomes the core of the Christian experience (cf.

Rom 8:15). The life of faith, as a filial existence, is the acknowledgment of a primordial and radical gift which upholds our lives. We see this clearly in Saint Paul's question to the Corinthians: "What have you that you did not receive?" (*1 Cor* 4:7). This was at the very heart of Paul's debate with the Pharisees: the issue of whether salvation is attained by faith or by the works of the law. Paul rejects the attitude of those who would consider themselves justified before God on the basis of their own works. Such people, even when they obey the commandments and do good works, are centred on themselves; they fail to realize that goodness comes from God. Those who live this way, who want to be the source of their own righteousness, find that the latter is soon depleted and that they are unable even to keep the law. They become closed in on themselves and isolated from the Lord and from others; their lives become futile and their works barren, like a tree far from water. Saint Augustine tells us in his usual concise and striking way: "*Ab eo qui fecit te, noli deficere nec ad te*", "Do not turn away from the one who made you, even to turn towards your- self".[15] Once I think that by turning away from God I will find myself, my life begins to fall apart (cf. *Lk* 15:11-24). The beginning of salvation is openness to something prior to ourselves, to a primordial gift that affirms life and sustains it in being. Only by being open to

---

[15] *De Continentia*, 4, 11: PL 40, 356.

and acknowledging this gift can we be transformed, experience sal- vation and bear good fruit. Salvation by faith means recognizing the primacy of God's gift. As Saint Paul puts it: "By grace you have been saved through faith, and this is not your own doing; it is the gift of God" (*Eph* 2:8).

20. Faith's new way of seeing things is centred on Christ. Faith in Christ brings salvation because in him our lives become radically open to a love that precedes us, a love that transforms us from within, acting in us and through us. This is clearly seen in Saint Paul's exegesis of a text from Deuteronomy, an exegesis consonant with the heart of the Old Testament message. Moses tells the people that God's command is neither too high nor too far away. There is no need to say: "Who will go up for us to heaven and bring it to us?" or "Who will go over the sea for us, and bring it to us?" (*Dt* 30:11-14). Paul interprets this nearness of God's word in terms of Christ's presence in the Christian. "Do not say in your heart, 'Who will ascend into heaven?' (that is, to bring Christ down), or 'Who will descend into the abyss?' (that is, to bring Christ up from the dead)" (*Rom* 10:6-7). Christ came down to earth and rose from the dead; by his incarnation and resurrection, the Son of God embraced the whole of human life and history, and now dwells in our hearts through the Holy Spirit. Faith knows that God has drawn close to us, that Christ has been given to us as a great gift which inwardly trans-

24

forms us, dwells within us and thus bestows on us the light that illumines the origin and the end of life.

21.   We come to see the difference, then, which faith makes for us. Those who believe are transformed by the love to which they have opened their hearts in faith. By their openness to this offer of primordial love, their lives are enlarged and expanded. "It is no longer I who live, but Christ who lives in me" (*Gal* 2:20). "May Christ dwell in your hearts through faith" (*Eph* 3:17). The self-awareness of the believer now expands because of the presence of another; it now lives in this other and thus, in love, life takes on a whole new breadth. Here we see the Holy Spirit at work. The Christian can see with the eyes of Jesus and share in his mind, his filial disposition, because he or she shares in his love, which is the Spirit. In the love of Jesus, we receive in a certain way his vision. Without being conformed to him in love, without the presence of the Spirit, it is impossible to confess him as Lord (cf. *1 Cor* 12:3).

The ecclesial form of faith

22.   In this way, the life of the believer becomes an ecclesial existence, a life lived in the Church. When Saint Paul tells the Christians of Rome that all who believe in Christ make up one body, he urges them not to boast of this; rather, each must think of himself "according to the measure of faith that God has assigned" (*Rom* 12:3).

Those who believe come to see themselves in the light of the faith which they profess: Christ is the mirror in which they find their own image fully realized. And just as Christ gathers to himself all those who believe and makes them his body, so the Christian comes to see himself as a member of this body, in an essential relationship with all other believers. The image of a body does not imply that the believer is simply one part of an anonymous whole, a mere cog in a great machine; rather, it brings out the vital union of Christ with believers, and of believers among themselves (cf. *Rom* 12:4-5). Christians are "one" (cf. *Gal* 3:28), yet in a way which does not make them lose their individuality; in service to others, they come into their own in the highest degree. This explains why, apart from this body, outside this unity of the Church in Christ, outside this Church which — in the words of Romano Guardini — "is the bearer within history of the plenary gaze of Christ on the world"[16] — faith loses its "measure"; it no longer finds its equilibrium, the space needed to sustain itself. Faith is necessarily ecclesial; it is professed from within the body of Christ as a concrete communion of believers. It is against this ecclesial backdrop that faith opens the individual Christian towards all others. Christ's word, once heard, by virtue of its inner power at work in the heart

[16] *"Vom Wesen katholischer Weltanschauung"* (1923), in *Unterscheidung des Christlichen. Gesammelte Studien 1923-1963*, Mainz, 1963, 24.

of the Christian, becomes a response, a spoken word, a profession of faith. As Saint Paul puts it: "one believes with the heart ... and confesses with the lips" (*Rom* 10:10). Faith is not a private matter, a completely individualistic notion or a personal opinion: it comes from hearing, and it is meant to find expression in words and to be proclaimed. For "how are they to believe in him of whom they have never heard? And how are they to hear without a preacher?" (*Rom* 10:14). Faith becomes operative in the Christian on the basis of the gift received, the love which attracts our hearts to Christ (cf. *Gal* 5:6), and enables us to become part of the Church's great pilgrimage through history until the end of the world. For those who have been transformed in this way, a new way of seeing opens up, faith becomes light for their eyes.

UNLESS YOU BELIEVE, YOU WILL NOT UNDERSTAND
(cf. *Is* 7:9)

Faith and truth

23.   Unless you believe, you will not understand (cf. *Is* 7:9). The Greek version of the Hebrew Bible, the Septuagint translation produced in Alexandria, gives the above rendering of the words spoken by the prophet Isaiah to King Ahaz. In this way, the issue of the knowledge of truth became central to faith. The Hebrew text, though, reads differently; the prophet says to the king: "If you will not believe, you shall not be established". Here there is a play on words, based on two forms of the verb *'amān*: "you will believe" (*ta'amînû*) and "you shall be established" (*tē'āmēnû*). Terrified by the might of his enemies, the king seeks the security that an alliance with the great Assyrian empire can offer. The prophet tells him instead to trust completely in the solid and steadfast rock which is the God of Israel. Because God is trustworthy, it is reasonable to have faith in him, to stand fast on his word. He is the same God that Isaiah will later call, twice in one verse, the God who is Amen, "the God of truth" (cf. *Is* 65:16), the enduring foundation of covenant fidelity. It might seem that the Greek version of the Bible, by translating "be established" as "understand", profoundly altered the

meaning of the text by moving away from the biblical notion of trust in God towards a Greek notion of intellectual understanding. Yet this translation, while certainly reflecting a dialogue with Hellenistic culture, is not alien to the underlying spirit of the Hebrew text. The firm foundation that Isaiah promises to the king is indeed grounded in an understanding of God's activity and the unity which he gives to human life and to the history of his people. The prophet challenges the king, and us, to understand the Lord's ways, seeing in God's faithfulness the wise plan which governs the ages. Saint Augustine took up this synthesis of the ideas of "understanding" and "being established" in his *Confessions* when he spoke of the truth on which one may rely in order to stand fast: "Then I shall be cast and set firm in the mould of your truth".[17] From the context we know that Augustine was concerned to show that this trustworthy truth of God is, as the Bible makes clear, his own faithful presence throughout history, his ability to hold together times and ages, and to gather into one the scattered strands of our lives.[18]

24. Read in this light, the prophetic text leads to one conclusion: we need knowledge, we need truth, because without these we cannot stand firm, we cannot move forward. Faith without truth does not save, it does not provide a sure

---

[17] XI, 30, 40: PL 32, 825.
[18] Cf. *ibid.*, 825-826.

footing. It remains a beautiful story, the projection of our deep yearning for happiness, something capable of satisfying us to the extent that we are willing to deceive ourselves. Either that, or it is reduced to a lofty sentiment which brings consolation and cheer, yet remains prey to the vagaries of our spirit and the changing seasons, incapable of sustaining a steady journey through life. If such were faith, King Ahaz would be right not to stake his life and the security of his kingdom on a feeling. But precisely because of its intrinsic link to truth, faith is instead able to offer a new light, superior to the king's calculations, for it sees further into the distance and takes into account the hand of God, who remains faithful to his covenant and his promises.

25.   Today more than ever, we need to be reminded of this bond between faith and truth, given the crisis of truth in our age. In contemporary culture, we often tend to consider the only real truth to be that of technology: truth is what we succeed in building and measuring by our scientific know-how, truth is what works and what makes life easier and more comfortable. Nowadays this appears as the only truth that is certain, the only truth that can be shared, the only truth that can serve as a basis for discussion or for common undertakings. Yet at the other end of the scale we are willing to allow for subjective truths of the individual, which consist in fidelity to his or her deepest convictions, yet these are

truths valid only for that individual and not capable of being proposed to others in an effort to serve the common good. But Truth itself, the truth which would comprehensively explain our life as individuals and in society, is regarded with suspicion. Surely this kind of truth — we hear it said — is what was claimed by the great totalitarian movements of the last century, a truth that imposed its own world view in order to crush the actual lives of individuals. In the end, what we are left with is relativism, in which the question of universal truth — and ultimately this means the question of God — is no longer relevant. It would be logical, from this point of view, to attempt to sever the bond between religion and truth, because it seems to lie at the root of fanaticism, which proves oppressive for anyone who does not share the same beliefs. In this regard, though, we can speak of a massive amnesia in our contemporary world. The question of truth is really a question of memory, deep memory, for it deals with something prior to ourselves and can succeed in uniting us in a way that transcends our petty and limited individual consciousness. It is a question about the origin of all that is, in whose light we can glimpse the goal and thus the meaning of our common path.

Knowledge of the truth and love

26. This being the case, can Christian faith provide a service to the common good with regard to the right way of understanding truth? To an-

swer this question, we need to reflect on the kind of knowledge involved in faith. Here a saying of Saint Paul can help us: "One believes with the heart" (*Rom* 10:10). In the Bible, the heart is the core of the human person, where all his or her different dimensions intersect: body and spirit, interiority and openness to the world and to others, intellect, will and affectivity. If the heart is capable of holding all these dimensions together, it is because it is where we become open to truth and love, where we let them touch us and deeply transform us. Faith transforms the whole person precisely to the extent that he or she becomes open to love. Through this blending of faith and love we come to see the kind of knowledge which faith entails, its power to convince and its ability to illumine our steps. Faith knows because it is tied to love, because love itself brings enlightenment. Faith's understanding is born when we receive the immense love of God which transforms us inwardly and enables us to see reality with new eyes.

27. The explanation of the connection between faith and certainty put forward by the philosopher Ludwig Wittgenstein is well known. For Wittgenstein, believing can be compared to the experience of falling in love: it is something subjective which cannot be proposed as a truth valid for everyone.[19] Indeed, most people nowadays

---

[19] Cf. *Vermischte Bemerkungen / Culture and Value*, ed. G.H. von Wright, Oxford, 1991, 32-33; 61-64.

would not consider love as related in any way to truth. Love is seen as an experience associated with the world of fleeting emotions, no longer with truth.

But is this an adequate description of love? Love cannot be reduced to an ephemeral emotion. True, it engages our affectivity, but in order to open it to the beloved and thus to blaze a trail leading away from self-centredness and towards another person, in order to build a lasting relationship, love aims at union with the beloved. Here we begin to see how love requires truth. Only to the extent that love is grounded in truth can it endure over time, can it transcend the passing moment and be sufficiently solid to sustain a shared journey. If love is not tied to truth, it falls prey to fickle emotions and cannot stand the test of time. True love, on the other hand, unifies all the elements of our person and becomes a new light pointing the way to a great and fulfilled life. Without truth, love is incapable of establishing a firm bond; it cannot liberate our isolated ego or redeem it from the fleeting moment in order to create life and bear fruit.

If love needs truth, truth also needs love. Love and truth are inseparable. Without love, truth becomes cold, impersonal and oppressive for people's day-to-day lives. The truth we seek, the truth that gives meaning to our journey through life, enlightens us whenever we are touched by love. One who loves realizes that love is an experience of truth, that it opens our

eyes to see reality in a new way, in union with the beloved. In this sense, Saint Gregory the Great could write that *"amor ipse notitia est"*, love is itself a kind of knowledge possessed of its own logic.[20] It is a relational way of viewing the world, which then becomes a form of shared knowledge, vision through the eyes of another and a shared vision of all that exists. William of Saint-Thierry, in the Middle Ages, follows this tradition when he comments on the verse of the Song of Songs where the lover says to the beloved, "Your eyes are doves" (*Song* 1:15).[21] The two eyes, says William, are faith-filled reason and love, which then become one in rising to the contemplation of God, when our understanding becomes "an understanding of enlightened love".[22]

28. This discovery of love as a source of knowledge, which is part of the primordial experience of every man and woman, finds authoritative expression in the biblical understanding of faith. In savouring the love by which God chose them and made them a people, Israel came to understand the overall unity of the divine plan. Faith-knowledge, because it is born of God's covenantal love, is knowledge which lights up a path in history. That is why, in the Bible, truth and fidelity go together: the true God is the God

---

[20] *Homiliae in Evangelia*, II, 27, 4: PL 76, 1207.
[21] Cf. *Expositio super Cantica Canticorum*, XVIII, 88: CCL, *Continuatio Mediaevalis* 87, 67.
[22] *Ibid.*, XIX, 90: CCL, *Continuatio Mediaevalis* 87, 69.

of fidelity who keeps his promises and makes possible, in time, a deeper understanding of his plan. Through the experience of the prophets, in the pain of exile and in the hope of a definitive return to the holy city, Israel came to see that this divine "truth" extended beyond the confines of its own history, to embrace the entire history of the world, beginning with creation. Faith-knowledge sheds light not only on the destiny of one particular people, but the entire history of the created world, from its origins to its consummation.

Faith as hearing and sight

29.   Precisely because faith-knowledge is linked to the covenant with a faithful God who enters into a relationship of love with man and speaks his word to him, the Bible presents it as a form of hearing; it is associated with the sense of hearing. Saint Paul would use a formula which became classic: *fides ex auditu*, "faith comes from hearing" (*Rom* 10:17). Knowledge linked to a word is always personal knowledge; it recognizes the voice of the one speaking, opens up to that person in freedom and follows him or her in obedience. Paul could thus speak of the "obedience of faith" (cf. *Rom* 1:5; 16:26).[23] Faith is

---

[23] "The obedience of faith (*Rom* 16:26; compare *Rom* 1:5, *2 Cor* 10:5-6) must be our response to the God who reveals. By faith one freely submits oneself entirely to God making the full submission of intellect and will to God who reveals, and willingly assenting to the revelation given by God. For this faith to be accorded, we need the grace of God, anticipating it and

also a knowledge bound to the passage of time, for words take time to be pronounced, and it is a knowledge assimilated only along a journey of discipleship. The experience of hearing can thus help to bring out more clearly the bond between knowledge and love.

At times, where knowledge of the truth is concerned, hearing has been opposed to sight; it has been claimed that an emphasis on sight was characteristic of Greek culture. If light makes possible that contemplation of the whole to which humanity has always aspired, it would also seem to leave no space for freedom, since it comes down from heaven directly to the eye, without calling for a response. It would also seem to call for a kind of static contemplation, far removed from the world of history with its joys and sufferings. From this standpoint, the biblical understanding of knowledge would be antithetical to the Greek understanding, inasmuch as the latter linked knowledge to sight in its attempt to attain a comprehensive understanding of reality.

This alleged antithesis does not, however, correspond to the biblical datum. The Old Testament combined both kinds of knowledge, since hearing God's word is accompanied by the desire

assisting it, as well as the interior helps of the Holy Spirit, who moves the heart and converts it to God, and opens the eyes of the mind and makes it easy for all to accept and believe the truth. The same Holy Spirit constantly perfects faith by his gifts, so that revelation may be more and more deeply understood" SECOND VATICAN ECUMENICAL COUNCIL, (Dogmatic Constitution on Divine Revelation *Dei Verbum*, 5).

to see his face. The ground was thus laid for a dialogue with Hellenistic culture, a dialogue present at the heart of sacred Scripture. Hearing emphasizes personal vocation and obedience, and the fact that truth is revealed in time. Sight provides a vision of the entire journey and allows it to be situated within God's overall plan; without this vision, we would be left only with unconnected parts of an unknown whole.

30. The bond between seeing and hearing in faith-knowledge is most clearly evident in John's Gospel. For the Fourth Gospel, to believe is both to hear and to see. Faith's hearing emerges as a form of knowing proper to love: it is a personal hearing, one which recognizes the voice of the Good Shepherd (cf. *Jn* 10:3-5); it is a hearing which calls for discipleship, as was the case with the first disciples: "Hearing him say these things, they followed Jesus" (*Jn* 1:37). But faith is also tied to sight. Seeing the signs which Jesus worked leads at times to faith, as in the case of the Jews who, following the raising of Lazarus, "having seen what he did, believed in him" (*Jn* 11:45). At other times, faith itself leads to deeper vision: "If you believe, you will see the glory of God" (*Jn* 11:40). In the end, belief and sight intersect: "Whoever believes in me believes in him who sent me. And whoever sees me sees him who sent me" (*Jn* 12:44-45). Joined to hearing, seeing then becomes a form of following Christ, and faith appears as a process of gazing,

in which our eyes grow accustomed to peering into the depths. Easter morning thus passes from John who, standing in the early morning darkness before the empty tomb, "saw and believed" (*Jn* 20:8), to Mary Magdalene who, after seeing Jesus (cf. *Jn* 20:14) and wanting to cling to him, is asked to contemplate him as he ascends to the Father, and finally to her full confession before the disciples: "I have seen the Lord!" (*Jn* 20:18).

How does one attain this synthesis between hearing and seeing? It becomes possible through the person of Christ himself, who can be seen and heard. He is the Word made flesh, whose glory we have seen (cf. *Jn* 1:14). The light of faith is the light of a countenance in which the Father is seen. In the Fourth Gospel, the truth which faith attains is the revelation of the Father in the Son, in his flesh and in his earthly deeds, a truth which can be defined as the "light-filled life" of Jesus.[24] This means that faith-knowledge does not direct our gaze to a purely inward truth. The truth which faith discloses to us is a truth centred on an encounter with Christ, on the contemplation of his life and on the awareness of his presence. Saint Thomas Aquinas speaks of the Apostles' *oculata fides* — a faith which sees! — in the presence of the body of the Risen Lord.[25] With their own eyes they saw the risen Jesus and

---

[24] Cf. H. SCHILIER, *Meditationen über den Johanneischen Begriff der Wahrheit*, in *Besinnung auf das Neue Testament. Exegetische Aufsätze und Vorträge 2*, Freiburg, Basel, Wien, 1959, 272.
[25] Cf. *S. Th.* III, q. 55, a. 2, ad 1.

they believed; in a word, they were able to peer into the depths of what they were seeing and to confess their faith in the Son of God, seated at the right hand of the Father.

31. It was only in this way, by taking flesh, by sharing our humanity, that the knowledge proper to love could come to full fruition. For the light of love is born when our hearts are touched and we open ourselves to the interior presence of the beloved, who enables us to recognize his mystery. Thus we can understand why, together with hearing and seeing, Saint John can speak of faith as touch, as he says in his First Letter: "What we have heard, what we have seen with our eyes and touched with our hands, concerning the word of life" (*1 Jn* 1:1). By his taking flesh and coming among us, Jesus has touched us, and through the sacraments he continues to touch us even today; transforming our hearts, he unceasingly enables us to acknowledge and acclaim him as the Son of God. In faith, we can touch him and receive the power of his grace. Saint Augustine, commenting on the account of the woman suffering from haemorrhages who touched Jesus and was cured (cf. *Lk* 8:45-46), says: "To touch him with our hearts: that is what it means to believe".[26] The crowd presses in on Jesus, but they do not reach him with the personal touch of faith, which apprehends the mystery that he is the Son who re-

---

[26] *Sermo* 229/L (Guelf. 14), 2 (Miscellanea Augustiniana 1, 487/488): *"Tangere autem corde, hoc est credere"*.

veals the Father. Only when we are configured to Jesus do we receive the eyes needed to see him.

The dialogue between faith and reason

32.   Christian faith, inasmuch as it proclaims the truth of God's total love and opens us to the power of that love, penetrates to the core of our human experience. Each of us comes to the light because of love, and each of us is called to love in order to remain in the light. Desirous of illumining all reality with the love of God made manifest in Jesus, and seeking to love others with that same love, the first Christians found in the Greek world, with its thirst for truth, an ideal partner in dialogue. The encounter of the Gospel message with the philosophical culture of the ancient world proved a decisive step in the evangelization of all peoples, and stimulated a fruitful interaction between faith and reason which has continued down the centuries to our own times. Blessed John Paul II, in his Encyclical Letter *Fides et Ratio*, showed how faith and reason each strengthen the other.[27] Once we discover the full light of Christ's love, we realize that each of the loves in our own lives had always contained a ray of that light, and we understand its ultimate destination. That fact that our human loves contain that ray of light also helps us to see how all love is meant to share in the complete self-gift of the

[27] Cf. Encyclical Letter *Fides et Ratio* (14 September 1998), 73: *AAS* (1999), 61-62.

Son of God for our sake. In this circular movement, the light of faith illumines all our human relationships, which can then be lived in union with the gentle love of Christ.

33.   In the life of Saint Augustine we find a significant example of this process whereby reason, with its desire for truth and clarity, was integrated into the horizon of faith and thus gained new understanding. Augustine accepted the Greek philosophy of light, with its insistence on the importance of sight. His encounter with Neoplatonism introduced him to the paradigm of the light which, descending from on high to illumine all reality, is a symbol of God. Augustine thus came to appreciate God's transcendence and discovered that all things have a certain transparency, that they can reflect God's goodness. This realization liberated him from his earlier Manichaeism, which had led him to think that good and evil were in constant conflict, confused and intertwined. The realization that God is light provided Augustine with a new direction in life and enabled him to acknowledge his sinfulness and to turn towards the good.

All the same, the decisive moment in Augustine's journey of faith, as he tells us in the *Confessions*, was not in the vision of a God above and beyond this world, but in an experience of hearing. In the garden, he heard a voice telling him: "Take and read". He then took up the book containing the epistles of Saint Paul and started

to read the thirteenth chapter of the Letter to the Romans.[28] In this way, the personal God of the Bible appeared to him: a God who is able to speak to us, to come down to dwell in our midst and to accompany our journey through history, making himself known in the time of hearing and response.

Yet this encounter with the God who speaks did not lead Augustine to reject light and seeing. He integrated the two perspectives of hearing and seeing, constantly guided by the revelation of God's love in Jesus. Thus Augustine developed a philosophy of light capable of embracing both the reciprocity proper to the word and the freedom born of looking to the light. Just as the word calls for a free response, so the light finds a response in the image which reflects it. Augustine can therefore associate hearing and seeing, and speak of "the word which shines forth within".[29] The light becomes, so to speak, the light of a word, because it is the light of a personal countenance, a light which, even as it enlightens us, calls us and seeks to be reflected on our faces and to shine from within us. Yet our longing for the vision of the whole, and not merely of fragments of history, remains and will be fulfilled in the end, when, as Augustine says, we will see and we will love.[30] Not because we will be able to

---

[28] Cf. *Confessiones*, VIII, 12, 29: PL 32, 762.
[29] *De Trinitate*, XV, 11, 20: PL 42, 1071: "*verbum quod intus lucet*".
[30] Cf. *De Civitate Dei*, XXII, 30, 5: PL 41, 804.

possess all the light, which will always be inexhaustible, but because we will enter wholly into that light.

34. The light of love proper to faith can illumine the questions of our own time about truth. Truth nowadays is often reduced to the subjective authenticity of the individual, valid only for the life of the individual. A common truth intimidates us, for we identify it with the intransigent demands of totalitarian systems. But if truth is a truth of love, if it is a truth disclosed in personal encounter with the Other and with others, then it can be set free from its enclosure in individuals and become part of the common good. As a truth of love, it is not one that can be imposed by force; it is not a truth that stifles the individual. Since it is born of love, it can penetrate to the heart, to the personal core of each man and woman. Clearly, then, faith is not intransigent, but grows in respectful coexistence with others. One who believes may not be presumptuous; on the contrary, truth leads to humility, since believers know that, rather than ourselves possessing truth, it is truth which embraces and possesses us. Far from making us inflexible, the security of faith sets us on a journey; it enables witness and dialogue with all.

Nor is the light of faith, joined to the truth of love, extraneous to the material world, for love is always lived out in body and spirit; the light of faith is an incarnate light radiating from the lumi-

nous life of Jesus. It also illumines the material world, trusts its inherent order and knows that it calls us to an ever widening path of harmony and understanding. The gaze of science thus benefits from faith: faith encourages the scientist to remain constantly open to reality in all its inexhaustible richness. Faith awakens the critical sense by preventing research from being satisfied with its own formulae and helps it to realize that nature is always greater. By stimulating wonder before the profound mystery of creation, faith broadens the horizons of reason to shed greater light on the world which discloses itself to scientific investigation.

Faith and the search for God

35.   The light of faith in Jesus also illumines the path of all those who seek God, and makes a specifically Christian contribution to dialogue with the followers of the different religions. The Letter to the Hebrews speaks of the witness of those just ones who, before the covenant with Abraham, already sought God in faith. Of Enoch "it was attested that he had pleased God" (*Heb* 11:5), something impossible apart from faith, for "whoever would approach God must believe that he exists and that he rewards those who seek him" (*Heb* 11:6). We can see from this that the path of religious man passes through the acknowledgment of a God who cares for us and is not impossible to find. What other reward can God give to those who seek him, if not to let himself be found? Even earlier, we encounter

Abel, whose faith was praised and whose gifts, his offering of the firstlings of his flock (cf. *Heb* 11:4), were therefore pleasing to God. Religious man strives to see signs of God in the daily experiences of life, in the cycle of the seasons, in the fruitfulness of the earth and in the movement of the cosmos. God is light and he can be found also by those who seek him with a sincere heart.

An image of this seeking can be seen in the Magi, who were led to Bethlehem by the star (cf. *Mt* 2:1-12). For them God's light appeared as a journey to be undertaken, a star which led them on a path of discovery. The star is a sign of God's patience with our eyes which need to grow accustomed to his brightness. Religious man is a wayfarer; he must be ready to let himself be led, to come out of himself and to find the God of perpetual surprises. This respect on God's part for our human eyes shows us that when we draw near to God, our human lights are not dissolved in the immensity of his light, as a star is engulfed by the dawn, but shine all the more brightly the closer they approach the primordial fire, like a mirror which reflects light. Christian faith in Jesus, the one Saviour of the world, proclaims that all God's light is concentrated in him, in his "luminous life" which discloses the origin and the end of history.[31] There is no human experience,

---

[31] Cf. CONGREGATION FOR THE DOCTRINE OF THE FAITH, Declaration *Dominus Iesus* (6 August 2000), 15: *AAS* 92 (2000), 756.

no journey of man to God, which cannot be taken up, illumined and purified by this light. The more Christians immerse themselves in the circle of Christ's light, the more capable they become of understanding and accompanying the path of every man and woman towards God.

Because faith is a way, it also has to do with the lives of those men and women who, though not believers, nonetheless desire to believe and continue to seek. To the extent that they are sincerely open to love and set out with whatever light they can find, they are already, even without knowing it, on the path leading to faith. They strive to act as if God existed, at times because they realize how important he is for finding a sure compass for our life in common or because they experience a desire for light amid darkness, but also because in perceiving life's grandeur and beauty they intuit that the presence of God would make it all the more beautiful. Saint Irenaeus of Lyons tells how Abraham, before hearing God's voice, had already sought him "in the ardent desire of his heart" and "went throughout the whole world, asking himself where God was to be found", until "God had pity on him who, all alone, had sought him in silence".[32] Anyone who sets off on the path of doing good to others is already drawing near to God, is already sustained by his help, for it is characteristic of the divine light to brighten our eyes whenever we walk towards the fullness of love.

[32] *Demonstratio Apostolicae Predicationis*, 24: SC 406, 117.

36.   Since faith is a light, it draws us into itself, inviting us to explore ever more fully the horizon which it illumines, all the better to know the object of our love. Christian theology is born of this desire. Clearly, theology is impossible without faith; it is part of the very process of faith, which seeks an ever deeper understanding of God's self-disclosure culminating in Christ. It follows that theology is more than simply an effort of human reason to analyze and understand, along the lines of the experimental sciences. God cannot be reduced to an object. He is a subject who makes himself known and perceived in an interpersonal relationship. Right faith orients reason to open itself to the light which comes from God, so that reason, guided by love of the truth, can come to a deeper knowledge of God. The great medieval theologians and teachers rightly held that theology, as a science of faith, is a participation in God's own knowledge of himself. It is not just our discourse about God, but first and foremost the acceptance and the pursuit of a deeper understanding of the word which God speaks to us, the word which God speaks about himself, for he is an eternal dialogue of communion, and he allows us to enter into this dialogue.[33] Theology thus demands the humili-

---

[33]   Cf. BONAVENTURE *Breviloquium, prol.*: Opera Omnia, V, Quaracchi 1891, 201; *In I Sent., proem*, q. 1, resp.: Opera Omnia, I, Quaracchi 1891, 7; , THOMAS AQUINAS, *S. Th* I, q.1.

ty to be "touched" by God, admitting its own limitations before the mystery, while striving to investigate, with the discipline proper to reason, the inexhaustible riches of this mystery.

Theology also shares in the ecclesial form of faith; its light is the light of the believing subject which is the Church. This implies, on the one hand, that theology must be at the service of the faith of Christians, that it must work humbly to protect and deepen the faith of everyone, especially ordinary believers. On the other hand, because it draws its life from faith, theology cannot consider the magisterium of the Pope and the bishops in communion with him as something extrinsic, a limitation of its freedom, but rather as one of its internal, constitutive dimensions, for the magisterium ensures our contact with the primordial source and thus provides the certainty of attaining to the word of Christ in all its integrity.

CHAPTER THREE

I DELIVERED TO YOU
WHAT I ALSO RECEIVED
(cf. *1 Cor* 15:3)

The Church, mother of our faith

37.　Those who have opened their hearts to God's love, heard his voice and received his light, cannot keep this gift to themselves. Since faith is hearing and seeing, it is also handed on as word and light. Addressing the Corinthians, Saint Paul used these two very images. On the one hand he says: "But just as we have the same spirit of faith that is in accordance with scripture — 'I believed, and so I spoke' — we also believe, and so we speak" (*2 Cor* 4:13). The word, once accepted, becomes a response, a confession of faith, which spreads to others and invites them to believe. Paul also uses the image of light: "All of us, with unveiled faces, seeing the glory of the Lord as though reflected in a mirror, are being transformed into the same image" (*2 Cor* 3:18). It is a light reflected from one face to another, even as Moses himself bore a reflection of God's glory after having spoken with him: "God... has shone in our hearts to give the light of the knowledge of the glory of God in the face of Christ" (*2 Cor* 4:6). The light of Christ shines, as in a mirror, upon the face of Christians; as it spreads, it comes down to us, so that we too can share in that vision and reflect that light to others, in

the same way that, in the Easter liturgy, the light of the paschal candle lights countless other candles. Faith is passed on, we might say, by contact, from one person to another, just as one candle is lighted from another. Christians, in their poverty, plant a seed so rich that it becomes a great tree, capable of filling the world with its fruit.

38. The transmission of the faith not only brings light to all men and women in every place; it travels through time, passing from one generation to another. Because faith is born of an encounter which takes place in history and lights up our journey through time, it must be passed on in every age. It is through an unbroken chain of witnesses that we come to see the face of Jesus. But how is this possible? How can we be certain, after all these centuries, that we have encountered the "real Jesus"? Were we merely isolated individuals, were our starting point simply our own individual ego seeking in itself the basis of absolutely sure knowledge, a certainty of this sort would be impossible. I cannot possibly verify for myself something which happened so long ago. But this is not the only way we attain knowledge. Persons always live in relationship. We come from others, we belong to others, and our lives are enlarged by our encounter with others. Even our own knowledge and self-awareness are relational; they are linked to others who have gone before us: in the first place, our parents, who gave us our life

and our name. Language itself, the words by which we make sense of our lives and the world around us, comes to us from others, preserved in the living memory of others. Self-knowledge is only possible when we share in a greater memory. The same thing holds true for faith, which brings human understanding to its fullness. Faith's past, that act of Jesus' love which brought new life to the world, comes down to us through the memory of others — witnesses — and is kept alive in that one remembering subject which is the Church. The Church is a Mother who teaches us to speak the language of faith. Saint John brings this out in his Gospel by close- ly uniting faith and memory and associating both with the working of the Holy Spirit, who, as Jesus says, "will remind you of all that I have said to you" (*Jn* 14:26). The love which is the Holy Spirit and which dwells in the Church unites ev- ery age and makes us contemporaries of Jesus, thus guiding us along our pilgrimage of faith.

39.   It is impossible to believe on our own. Faith is not simply an individual decision which takes place in the depths of the believer's heart, nor a completely private relationship between the "I" of the believer and the divine "Thou", between an autonomous subject and God. By its very na- ture, faith is open to the "We" of the Church; it always takes place within her communion. We are reminded of this by the dialogical format of the creed used in the baptismal liturgy. Our belief is expressed in response to an invitation, to a word

which must be heard and which is not my own; it exists as part of a dialogue and cannot be merely a profession originating in an individual. We can respond in the singular — "I believe" — only because we are part of a greater fellowship, only because we also say "We believe". This openness to the ecclesial "We" reflects the openness of God's own love, which is not only a relationship between the Father and the Son, between an "I" and a "Thou", but is also, in the Spirit, a "We", a communion of persons. Here we see why those who believe are never alone, and why faith tends to spread, as it invites others to share in its joy. Those who receive faith discover that their horizons expand as new and enriching relationships come to life. Tertullian puts this well when he describes the catechumens who, "after the cleansing which gives new birth" are welcomed into the house of their mother and, as part of a new family, pray the Our Father together with their brothers and sisters.[34]

The sacraments and the transmission of faith

40. The Church, like every family, passes on to her children the whole store of her memories. But how does this come about in a way that nothing is lost, but rather everything in the patrimony of faith comes to be more deeply understood? It is through the apostolic Tradition preserved in the

[34] Cf. *De Baptismo*, 20, 5: CCL 1, 295.

Church with the assistance of the Holy Spirit that we enjoy a living contact with the foundational memory. What was handed down by the apostles — as the Second Vatican Council states — "comprises everything that serves to make the people of God live their lives in holiness and increase their faith. In this way the Church, in her doctrine, life and worship, perpetuates and transmits to every generation all that she herself is, all that she believes".[35]

Faith, in fact, needs a setting in which it can be witnessed to and communicated, a means which is suitable and proportionate to what is communicated. For transmitting a purely doctrinal content, an idea might suffice, or perhaps a book, or the repetition of a spoken message. But what is communicated in the Church, what is handed down in her living Tradition, is the new light born of an encounter with the true God, a light which touches us at the core of our being and engages our minds, wills and emotions, opening us to relationships lived in communion. There is a special means for passing down this fullness, a means capable of engaging the entire person, body and spirit, interior life and relationships with others. It is the sacraments, celebrated in the Church's liturgy. The sacraments communicate an incarnate memory, linked to the times and places of our lives, linked to all our senses; in

---

[35] Dogmatic Constitution on Divine Revelation *Dei Verbum*, 8.

them the whole person is engaged as a member of a living subject and part of a network of communitarian relationships. While the sacraments are indeed sacraments of faith,[36] it can also be said that faith itself possesses a sacramental structure. The awakening of faith is linked to the dawning of a new sacramental sense in our lives as human beings and as Christians, in which visible and material realities are seen to point beyond themselves to the mystery of the eternal.

41.   The transmission of faith occurs first and foremost in baptism. Some might think that baptism is merely a way of symbolizing the confession of faith, a pedagogical tool for those who require images and signs, while in itself ultimately unnecessary. An observation of Saint Paul about baptism reminds us that this is not the case. Paul states that "we were buried with him by baptism into death, so that, just as Christ was raised from the dead by the glory of the Father, we too might walk in newness of life" (*Rom* 6:4). In baptism we become a new creation and God's adopted children. The Apostle goes on to say that Christians have been entrusted to a "standard of teaching" (*týpos didachés*), which they now obey from the heart (cf. *Rom* 6:17). In baptism we receive both a teaching to be professed and a specific way of life which demands the engagement of the whole person and sets us on the path

---

[36]   Cf. SECOND VATICAN ECUMENICAL COUNCIL, Constitution on the Sacred Liturgy *Sacrosanctum Concilium*, 59.

to goodness. Those who are baptized are set in a new context, entrusted to a new environment, a new and shared way of acting, in the Church. Baptism makes us see, then, that faith is not the achievement of isolated individuals; it is not an act which someone can perform on his own, but rather something which must be received by entering into the ecclesial communion which transmits God's gift. No one baptizes himself, just as no one comes into the world by himself. Baptism is something we receive.

42. What are the elements of baptism which introduce us into this new "standard of teaching"? First, the name of the Trinity — the Father, the Son and the Holy Spirit — is invoked upon the catechumen. Thus, from the outset, a synthesis of the journey of faith is provided. The God who called Abraham and wished to be called his God, the God who revealed his name to Moses, the God who, in giving us his Son, revealed fully the mystery of his Name, now bestows upon the baptized a new filial identity. This is clearly seen in the act of baptism itself: immersion in water. Water is at once a symbol of death, inviting us to pass through self-conversion to a new and greater identity, and a symbol of life, of a womb in which we are reborn by following Christ in his new life. In this way, through immersion in water, baptism speaks to us of the incarnational structure of faith. Christ's work penetrates the depths of our being and transforms us radically, making

us adopted children of God and sharers in the divine nature. It thus modifies all our relationships, our place in this world and in the universe, and opens them to God's own life of communion. This change which takes place in baptism helps us to appreciate the singular importance of the catechumenate — whereby growing numbers of adults, even in societies with ancient Christian roots, now approach the sacrament of baptism — for the new evangelization. It is the road of preparation for baptism, for the transformation of our whole life in Christ.

To appreciate this link between baptism and faith, we can recall a text of the prophet Isaiah, which was associated with baptism in early Christian literature: "Their refuge will be the fortresses of rocks... their water assured" (*Is* 33:16).[37] The baptized, rescued from the waters of death, were now set on a "fortress of rock" because they had found a firm and reliable foundation. The waters of death were thus transformed into waters of life. The Greek text, in speaking of that water which is "assured", uses the word *pistós*, "faithful". The waters of baptism are indeed faithful and trustworthy, for they flow with the power of Christ's love, the source of our assurance in the journey of life.

43. The structure of baptism, its form as a rebirth in which we receive a new name and a new

---

[37] Cf. *Epistula Barnabae*, 11, 5: SC 172, 162

life, helps us to appreciate the meaning and importance of infant baptism. Children are not capable of accepting the faith by a free act, nor are they yet able to profess that faith on their own; therefore the faith is professed by their parents and godparents in their name. Since faith is a reality lived within the community of the Church, part of a common "We", children can be supported by others, their parents and godparents, and welcomed into their faith, which is the faith of the Church; this is symbolized by the candle which the child's father lights from the paschal candle. The structure of baptism, then, demonstrates the critical importance of cooperation between Church and family in passing on the faith. Parents are called, as Saint Augustine once said, not only to bring children into the world but also to bring them to God, so that through baptism they can be reborn as children of God and receive the gift of faith.[38] Thus, along with life, children are given a fundamental orientation and assured of a good future; this orientation will be further strengthened in the sacrament of Confirmation with the seal of the Holy Spirit.

44.   The sacramental character of faith finds its highest expression in the Eucharist. The Eucharist is a precious nourishment for faith: an encounter with Christ truly present in the supreme

---

[38] Cf. *De Nuptiis et Concupiscentia* I, 4, 5: PL 44, 413: "*Habent quippe intentionem generandi regenerandos, ut qui ex eis saeculi filii nascuntur in Dei filios renascantur*".

act of his love, the life-giving gift of himself. In the Eucharist we find the intersection of faith's two dimensions. On the one hand, there is the dimension of history: the Eucharist is an act of remembrance, a making present of the mystery in which the past, as an event of death and resurrection, demonstrates its ability to open up a future, to foreshadow ultimate fulfilment. The liturgy reminds us of this by its repetition of the word *hodie*, the "today" of the mysteries of salvation. On the other hand, we also find the dimension which leads from the visible world to the invisible. In the Eucharist we learn to see the heights and depths of reality. The bread and wine are changed into the body and blood of Christ, who becomes present in his passover to the Father: this movement draws us, body and soul, into the movement of all creation towards its fulfilment in God.

45.   In the celebration of the sacraments, the Church hands down her memory especially through the profession of faith. The creed does not only involve giving one's assent to a body of abstract truths; rather, when it is recited the whole of life is drawn into a journey towards full communion with the living God. We can say that in the creed believers are invited to enter into the mystery which they profess and to be transformed by it. To understand what this means, let us look first at the contents of the creed. It has a trinitarian structure: the Father and the Son

are united in the Spirit of love. The believer thus states that the core of all being, the inmost secret of all reality, is the divine communion. The creed also contains a christological confession: it takes us through all the mysteries of Christ's life up to his death, resurrection and ascension into heaven before his final return in glory. It tells us that this God of communion, reciprocal love between the Father and the Son in the Spirit, is capable of embracing all of human history and drawing it into the dynamic unity of the Godhead, which has its source and fulfillment in the Father. The believer who professes his or her faith is taken up, as it were, into the truth being professed. He or she cannot truthfully recite the words of the creed without being changed, without becoming part of that history of love which embraces us and expands our being, making it part of a great fellowship, the ultimate subject which recites the creed, namely, the Church. All the truths in which we believe point to the mystery of the new life of faith as a journey of communion with the living God.

Faith, prayer and the Decalogue

46. Two other elements are essential in the faithful transmission of the Church's memory. First, the Lord's Prayer, the "Our Father". Here Christians learn to share in Christ's own spiritual experience and to see all things through his eyes. From him who is light from light, the only-begotten Son of the Father, we come to know

God and can thus kindle in others the desire to draw near to him.

Similarly important is the link between faith and the Decalogue. Faith, as we have said, takes the form of a journey, a path to be followed, which begins with an encounter with the living God. It is in the light of faith, of complete entrustment to the God who saves, that the Ten Commandments take on their deepest truth, as seen in the words which introduce them: "I am the Lord your God, who brought you out of the land of Egypt" (*Ex* 20:2). The Decalogue is not a set of negative commands, but concrete directions for emerging from the desert of the selfish and self-enclosed ego in order to enter into dialogue with God, to be embraced by his mercy and then to bring that mercy to others. Faith thus professes the love of God, origin and upholder of all things, and lets itself be guided by this love in order to journey towards the fullness of communion with God. The Decalogue appears as the path of gratitude, the response of love, made possible because in faith we are receptive to the experience of God's transforming love for us. And this path receives new light from Jesus' teaching in the Sermon on the Mount (cf. *Mt* 5-7).

These, then, are the four elements which comprise the storehouse of memory which the Church hands down: the profession of faith, the celebration of the sacraments, the path of the ten commandments, and prayer. The Church's catechesis has traditionally been structured around these four elements; this includes the *Catechism of*

the Catholic Church, which is a fundamental aid for that unitary act with which the Church communicates the entire content of her faith: "all that she herself is, and all that she believes".[39]

The unity and integrity of faith

47.   The unity of the Church in time and space is linked to the unity of the faith: "there is one body and one Spirit… one faith" (*Eph* 4:4-5). These days we can imagine a group of people being united in a common cause, in mutual affection, in sharing the same destiny and a single purpose. But we find it hard to conceive of a unity in one truth. We tend to think that a unity of this sort is incompatible with freedom of thought and personal autonomy. Yet the experience of love shows us that a common vision is possible, for through love we learn how to see reality through the eyes of others, not as something which impoverishes but instead enriches our vision. Genuine love, after the fashion of God's love, ultimately requires truth, and the shared contemplation of the truth which is Jesus Christ enables love to become deep and enduring. This is also the great joy of faith: a unity of vision in one body and one spirit. Saint Leo the Great could say: "If faith is not one, then it is not faith".[40]

---

[39], SECOND VATICAN ECUMENICAL COUNCIL, Dogmatic Constitution on Divine Revelation *Dei Verbum*, 8.

[40] *In Nativitate Domini Sermo*, 4, 6: SC 22, 110.

What is the secret of this unity? Faith is "one", in the first place, because of the oneness of the God who is known and confessed. All the articles of faith speak of God; they are ways to know him and his works. Consequently, their unity is far superior to any possible construct of human reason. They possess a unity which enriches us because it is given to us and makes us one.

Faith is also one because it is directed to the one Lord, to the life of Jesus, to the concrete history which he shares with us. Saint Irenaeus of Lyons made this clear in his struggle against Gnosticism. The Gnostics held that there are two kinds of faith: a crude, imperfect faith suited to the masses, which remained at the level of Jesus' flesh and the contemplation of his mysteries; and a deeper, perfect faith reserved to a small circle of initiates who were intellectually capable of rising above the flesh of Jesus towards the mysteries of the unknown divinity. In opposition to this claim, which even today exerts a certain attraction and has its followers, Saint Irenaeus insisted that there is but one faith, for it is grounded in the concrete event of the incarnation and can never transcend the flesh and history of Christ, inasmuch as God willed to reveal himself fully in that flesh. For this reason, he says, there is no difference in the faith of "those able to discourse of it at length" and "those who speak but little", between the greater and the less: the first cannot increase the faith, nor the second diminish it.[41]

---

[41] Cf. IRENAEUS, *Adversus Haereses,* , I, 10, 2: SC 264, 160.

Finally, faith is one because it is shared by the whole Church, which is one body and one Spirit. In the communion of the one subject which is the Church, we receive a common gaze. By professing the same faith, we stand firm on the same rock, we are transformed by the same Spirit of love, we radiate one light and we have a single insight into reality.

48.   Since faith is one, it must be professed in all its purity and integrity. Precisely because all the articles of faith are interconnected, to deny one of them, even of those that seem least important, is tantamount to distorting the whole. Each period of history can find this or that point of faith easier or harder to accept: hence the need for vigilance in ensuring that the deposit of faith is passed on in its entirety (cf. *1 Tim* 6:20) and that all aspects of the profession of faith are duly emphasized. Indeed, inasmuch as the unity of faith is the unity of the Church, to subtract something from the faith is to subtract something from the veracity of communion. The Fathers described faith as a body, the body of truth composed of various members, by analogy with the body of Christ and its prolongation in the Church.[42] The integrity of the faith was also tied to the image of the Church as a virgin and her fidelity in love for Christ her spouse; harming the faith means harming communion with the Lord.[43] The unity

---

[42] Cf. *ibid.*, II, 27, 1: SC 294, 264.
[43] Cf. AUGUSTINE, *De Sancta Virginitate*, 48, 48: PL 40, 424-

of faith, then, is the unity of a living body; this was clearly brought out by Blessed John Henry Newman when he listed among the characteristic notes for distinguishing the continuity of doctrine over time its power to assimilate everything that it meets in the various settings in which it becomes present and in the diverse cultures which it encounters,[44] purifying all things and bringing them to their finest expression. Faith is thus shown to be universal, catholic, because its light expands in order to illumine the entire cosmos and all of history.

49. As a service to the unity of faith and its integral transmission, the Lord gave his Church the gift of apostolic succession. Through this means, the continuity of the Church's memory is ensured and certain access can be had to the wellspring from which faith flows. The assurance of continuity with the origins is thus given by living persons, in a way consonant with the living faith which the Church is called to transmit. She depends on the fidelity of witnesses chosen by the Lord for this task. For this reason, the magisterium always speaks in obedience to the prior word on which faith is based; it is reliable because of its trust in the word which it hears, preserves

425: *"Servatur et in fide inviolata quaedam castitas virginalis, qua Eccle- sia uni viro virgo casta coaptatur"*.
    [44] Cf. *An Essay on the Development of Christian Doctrine* (Uniform Edition: Longmans, Green and Company, London, 1868-1881), 185-189.

and expounds.[45] In Saint Paul's farewell discourse to the elders of Ephesus at Miletus, which Saint Luke recounts for us in the Acts of the Apostles, he testifies that he had carried out the task which the Lord had entrusted to him of "declaring the whole counsel of God" (*Acts* 20:27). Thanks to the Church's magisterium, this counsel can come to us in its integrity, and with it the joy of being able to follow it fully.

---

[45] Cf. SECOND VATICAN COUNCIL, Dogmatic Constitution on Divine Revelation *Dei Verbum*, 10.

GOD PREPARES A CITY FOR THEM
(cf. *Heb* 11:16)

Faith and the common good

50.   In presenting the story of the patriarchs and the righteous men and women of the Old Testament, the Letter to the Hebrews highlights an essential aspect of their faith. That faith is not only presented as a journey, but also as a process of building, the preparing of a place in which human beings can dwell together with one another. The first builder was Noah who saved his family in the ark (*Heb* 11:7). Then comes Abraham, of whom it is said that by faith he dwelt in tents, as he looked forward to the city with firm foundations (cf. *Heb* 11:9-10). With faith comes a new reliability, a new firmness, which God alone can give. If the man of faith finds support in the God of fidelity, the God who is Amen (cf. *Is* 65:16), and thus becomes firm himself, we can now also say that firmness of faith marks the city which God is preparing for mankind. Faith reveals just how firm the bonds between people can be when God is present in their midst. Faith does not merely grant interior firmness, a steadfast conviction on the part of the believer; it also sheds light on every human relationship because it is born of love and reflects God's own love. The God who is himself reliable gives us a city which is reliable.

51.   Precisely because it is linked to love (cf. *Gal* 5:6), the light of faith is concretely placed at the service of justice, law and peace. Faith is born of an encounter with God's primordial love, wherein the meaning and goodness of our life become evident; our life is illumined to the extent that it enters into the space opened by that love, to the extent that it becomes, in other words, a path and praxis leading to the fullness of love. The light of faith is capable of enhancing the richness of human relations, their ability to endure, to be trustworthy, to enrich our life together. Faith does not draw us away from the world or prove irrelevant to the concrete concerns of the men and women of our time. Without a love which is trustworthy, nothing could truly keep men and women united. Human unity would be conceivable only on the basis of utility, on a calculus of conflicting interests or on fear, but not on the goodness of living together, not on the joy which the mere presence of others can give. Faith makes us appreciate the architecture of human relationships because it grasps their ultimate foundation and definitive destiny in God, in his love, and thus sheds light on the art of building; as such it becomes a service to the common good. Faith is truly a good for everyone; it is a common good. Its light does not simply brighten the interior of the Church, nor does it serve solely to build an eternal city in the hereafter; it helps us build our societies in such a way that they can journey towards a future of hope. The Letter to the

Hebrews offers an example in this regard when it names, among the men and women of faith, Samuel and David, whose faith enabled them to "administer justice" (*Heb* 11:33). This expression refers to their justice in governance, to that wisdom which brings peace to the people (cf. *1 Sam* 12:3-5; *2 Sam* 8:15). The hands of faith are raised up to heaven, even as they go about building in charity a city based on relationships in which the love of God is laid as a foundation.

Faith and the family

52.   In Abraham's journey towards the future city, the Letter to the Hebrews mentions the blessing which was passed on from fathers to sons (cf. *Heb* 11:20-21). The first setting in which faith enlightens the human city is the family. I think first and foremost of the stable union of man and woman in marriage. This union is born of their love, as a sign and presence of God's own love, and of the acknowledgment and acceptance of the goodness of sexual differentiation, whereby spouses can become one flesh (cf. *Gen* 2:24) and are enabled to give birth to a new life, a manifestation of the Creator's goodness, wisdom and loving plan. Grounded in this love, a man and a woman can promise each other mutual love in a gesture which engages their entire lives and mirrors many features of faith. Promising love for ever is possible when we perceive a plan bigger than our own ideas and undertakings, a plan which sustains us and enables

us to surrender our future entirely to the one we love. Faith also helps us to grasp in all its depth and richness the begetting of children, as a sign of the love of the Creator who entrusts us with the mystery of a new person. So it was that Sarah, by faith, became a mother, for she trusted in God's fidelity to his promise (cf. *Heb* 11:11).

53. In the family, faith accompanies every age of life, beginning with childhood: children learn to trust in the love of their parents. This is why it is so important that within their families parents encourage shared expressions of faith which can help children gradually to mature in their own faith. Young people in particular, who are going through a period in their lives which is so complex, rich and important for their faith, ought to feel the constant closeness and support of their families and the Church in their journey of faith. We have all seen, during World Youth Days, the joy that young people show in their faith and their desire for an ever more solid and generous life of faith. Young people want to live life to the fullest. Encountering Christ, letting themselves be caught up in and guided by his love, enlarges the horizons of existence, gives it a firm hope which will not disappoint. Faith is no refuge for the fainthearted, but something which enhances our lives. It makes us aware of a magnificent calling, the vocation of love. It assures us that this love is trustworthy and worth embracing, for it is based on God's faithfulness which is stronger than our every weakness.

54.   Absorbed and deepened in the family, faith becomes a light capable of illumining all our relationships in society. As an experience of the mercy of God the Father, it sets us on the path of brotherhood. Modernity sought to build a universal brotherhood based on equality, yet we gradually came to realize that this brotherhood, lacking a reference to a common Father as its ultimate foundation, cannot endure. We need to return to the true basis of brotherhood. The history of faith has been from the beginning a history of brotherhood, albeit not without conflict. God calls Abraham to go forth from his land and promises to make of him a great nation, a great people on whom the divine blessing rests (cf. *Gen* 12:1-3). As salvation history progresses, it becomes evident that God wants to make everyone share as brothers and sisters in that one blessing, which attains its fullness in Jesus, so that all may be one. The boundless love of our Father also comes to us, in Jesus, through our brothers and sisters. Faith teaches us to see that every man and woman represents a blessing for me, that the light of God's face shines on me through the faces of my brothers and sisters.

How many benefits has the gaze of Christian faith brought to the city of men for their common life! Thanks to faith we have come to understand the unique dignity of each person, something which was not clearly seen in antiquity. In the second century the pagan Celsus

reproached Christians for an idea that he considered foolishness and delusion: namely, that God created the world for man, setting human beings at the pinnacle of the entire cosmos. "Why claim that [grass] grows for the benefit of man, rather than for that of the most savage of the brute beasts?"[46] "If we look down to Earth from the heights of heaven, would there really be any difference between our activities and those of the ants and bees?"[47] At the heart of biblical faith is God's love, his concrete concern for every person, and his plan of salvation which embraces all of humanity and all creation, culminating in the incarnation, death and resurrection of Jesus Christ. Without insight into these realities, there is no criterion for discerning what makes human life precious and unique. Man loses his place in the universe, he is cast adrift in nature, either renouncing his proper moral responsibility or else presuming to be a sort of absolute judge, endowed with an unlimited power to manipulate the world around him.

55.   Faith, on the other hand, by revealing the love of God the Creator, enables us to respect nature all the more, and to discern in it a grammar written by the hand of God and a dwelling place entrusted to our protection and care. Faith also helps us to devise models of development which are based not simply on utility and prof-

[46] ORIGEN, *Contra Celsum*, IV, 75: SC 136, 372.
[47] *Ibid.*, 85: SC 136, 394.

it, but consider creation as a gift for which we are all indebted; it teaches us to create just forms of government, in the realization that authority comes from God and is meant for the service of the common good. Faith likewise offers the possibility of forgiveness, which so often demands time and effort, patience and commitment. Forgiveness is possible once we discover that goodness is always prior to and more powerful than evil, and that the word with which God affirms our life is deeper than our every denial. From a purely anthropological standpoint, unity is superior to conflict; rather than avoiding conflict, we need to confront it in an effort to resolve and move beyond it, to make it a link in a chain, as part of a progress towards unity.

When faith is weakened, the foundations of life also risk being weakened, as the poet T.S. Eliot warned: "Do you need to be told that even those modest attainments / As you can boast in the way of polite society / Will hardly survive the Faith to which they owe their significance?"[48] If we remove faith in God from our cities, mutual trust would be weakened, we would remain united only by fear and our stability would be threatened. In the Letter to the Hebrews we read that "God is not ashamed to be called their God; indeed, he has prepared a city for them" (*Heb* 11:16). Here the expression "is

---

[48] "Choruses from *The Rock*", in *The Collected Poems and Plays 1909-1950*, New York, 1980, 106.

not ashamed" is associated with public acknowledgment. The intention is to say that God, by his concrete actions, makes a public avowal that he is present in our midst and that he desires to solidify every human relationship. Could it be the case, instead, that we are the ones who are ashamed to call God our God? That we are the ones who fail to confess him as such in our public life, who fail to propose the grandeur of the life in common which he makes possible? Faith illumines life and society. If it possesses a creative light for each new moment of history, it is because it sets every event in relationship to the origin and destiny of all things in the Father.

Consolation and strength amid suffering

56.   Writing to the Christians of Corinth about his sufferings and tribulations, Saint Paul links his faith to his preaching of the Gospel. In himself he sees fulfilled the passage of Scripture which reads: "I believed, and so I spoke" (*2 Cor* 4:13). The reference is to a verse of Psalm 116, in which the psalmist exclaims: "I kept my faith, even when I said, 'I am greatly afflicted'" (v. 10). To speak of faith often involves speaking of painful testing, yet it is precisely in such testing that Paul sees the most convincing proclamation of the Gospel, for it is in weakness and suffering that we discover God's power which triumphs over our weakness and suffering. The apostle himself experienced a dying which would become life for Christians (cf. *2 Cor* 4:7-12). In the hour of

trial faith brings light, while suffering and weakness make it evident that "we do not proclaim ourselves; we proclaim Jesus Christ as Lord" (*2 Cor* 4:5). The eleventh chapter of the Letter to the Hebrews concludes with a reference to those who suffered for their faith (cf. *Heb* 11:35-38); outstanding among these was Moses, who suffered abuse for the Christ (cf. v. 26). Christians know that suffering cannot be eliminated, yet it can have meaning and become an act of love and entrustment into the hands of God who does not abandon us; in this way it can serve as a moment of growth in faith and love. By contemplating Christ's union with the Father even at the height of his sufferings on the cross (cf. *Mk* 15:34), Christians learn to share in the same gaze of Jesus. Even death is illumined and can be experienced as the ultimate call to faith, the ultimate "Go forth from your land" (*Gen* 12:1), the ultimate "Come!" spoken by the Father, to whom we abandon ourselves in the confidence that he will keep us steadfast even in our final passage.

57. Nor does the light of faith make us forget the sufferings of this world. How many men and women of faith have found mediators of light in those who suffer! So it was with Saint Francis of Assisi and the leper, or with Blessed Mother Teresa of Calcutta and her poor. They understood the mystery at work in them. In drawing near to the suffering, they were certainly not able to eliminate

all their pain or to explain every evil. Faith is not a light which scatters all our darkness, but a lamp which guides our steps in the night and suffices for the journey. To those who suffer, God does not provide arguments which explain everything; rather, his response is that of an accompanying presence, a history of goodness which touches every story of suffering and opens up a ray of light. In Christ, God himself wishes to share this path with us and to offer us his gaze so that we might see the light within it. Christ is the one who, having endured suffering, is "the pioneer and perfecter of our faith" (*Heb* 12:2).

Suffering reminds us that faith's service to the common good is always one of hope — a hope which looks ever ahead in the knowledge that only from God, from the future which comes from the risen Jesus, can our society find solid and lasting foundations. In this sense faith is linked to hope, for even if our dwelling place here below is wasting away, we have an eternal dwelling place which God has already prepared in Christ, in his body (cf. *2 Cor* 4:16-5:5). The dynamic of faith, hope and charity (cf. *1 Th* 1:3; *1 Cor* 13:13) thus leads us to embrace the concerns of all men and women on our journey towards that city "whose architect and builder is God" (*Heb* 11:10), for "hope does not disappoint" (*Rom* 5:5).

In union with faith and charity, hope propels us towards a sure future, set against a different horizon with regard to the illusory enticements

of the idols of this world yet granting new momentum and strength to our daily lives. Let us refuse to be robbed of hope, or to allow our hope to be dimmed by facile answers and solutions which block our progress, "fragmenting" time and changing it into space. Time is always much greater than space. Space hardens processes, whereas time propels towards the future and encourages us to go forward in hope.

BLESSED IS SHE WHO BELIEVED (*Lk* 1:45)

58.   In the parable of the sower, Saint Luke has left us these words of the Lord about the "good soil": "These are the ones who when they hear the word, hold it fast in an honest and good heart, and bear fruit with patience endurance" (*Lk* 8:15). In the context of Luke's Gospel, this mention of an honest and good heart which hears and keeps the word is an implicit portrayal of the faith of the Virgin Mary. The evangelist himself speaks of Mary's memory, how she treasured in her heart all that she had heard and seen, so that the word could bear fruit in her life. The Mother of the Lord is the perfect icon of faith; as Saint Elizabeth would say: "Blessed is she who believed" (*Lk* 1:45).

In Mary, the Daughter of Zion, is fulfilled the long history of faith of the Old Testament, with its account of so many faithful women, beginning with Sarah: women who, alongside the patriarchs, were those in whom God's promise

was fulfilled and new life flowered. In the fullness of time, God's word was spoken to Mary and she received that word into her heart, her entire being, so that in her womb it could take flesh and be born as light for humanity. Saint Justin Martyr, in his dialogue with Trypho, uses a striking expression; he tells us that Mary, receiving the message of the angel, conceived "faith and joy".[49] In the Mother of Jesus, faith demonstrated its fruitfulness; when our own spiritual lives bear fruit we become filled with joy, which is the clearest sign of faith's grandeur. In her own life Mary completed the pilgrimage of faith, following in the footsteps of her Son.[50] In her the faith journey of the Old Testament was thus taken up into the following of Christ and transformed by him, entering into the gaze of the incarnate Son of God.

59.   We can say that in the Blessed Virgin Mary we find something I mentioned earlier, namely that the believer is completely taken up into his or her confession of faith. Because of her close bond with Jesus, Mary is strictly connected to what we believe. As Virgin and Mother, Mary offers us a clear sign of Christ's divine sonship. The eternal origin of Christ is in the Father. He is the Son in a total and unique sense, and so he is born in time without the intervention of

---

[49]   Cf. *Dialogus cum Tryphone Iudaeo*, 100, 5: PG 6, 710.
[50]   Cf. SECOND VATICAN COUNCIL, Dogmatic Constitution on the Church *Lumen Gentium*, 58.

a man. As the Son, Jesus brings to the world a new beginning and a new light, the fullness of God's faithful love bestowed on humanity. But Mary's true motherhood also ensured for the Son of God an authentic human history, true flesh in which he would die on the cross and rise from the dead. Mary would accompany Jesus to the cross (cf. *Jn* 19:25), whence her motherhood would extend to each of his disciples (cf. *Jn* 19:26-27). She will also be present in the upper room after Jesus' resurrection and ascension, joining the apostles in imploring the gift of the Spirit (cf. *Acts* 1:14). The movement of love between Father, Son and Spirit runs through our history, and Christ draws us to himself in order to save us (cf. *Jn* 12:32). At the centre of our faith is the confession of Jesus, the Son of God, born of a woman, who brings us, through the gift of the Holy Spirit, to adoption as sons and daughters (cf. *Gal* 4:4).

60.   Let us turn in prayer to Mary, Mother of the Church and Mother of our faith.

Mother, help our faith!

Open our ears to hear God's word and to recognize his voice and call.

Awaken in us a desire to follow in his footsteps, to go forth from our own land and to receive his promise.

Help us to be touched by his love, that we may touch him in faith.

Help us to entrust ourselves fully to him and to believe in his love, especially at times of trial,

beneath the shadow of the cross, when our faith is called to mature.

Sow in our faith the joy of the Risen One.

Remind us that those who believe are never alone.

Teach us to see all things with the eyes of Jesus, that he may be light for our path. And may this light of faith always increase in us, until the dawn of that undying day which is Christ himself, your Son, our Lord!

Given in Rome, at Saint Peter's, on 29 June, the Solemnity of the Holy Apostles Peter and Paul, in the year 2013, the first of my pontificate.

Franciscus

the WORD
among us ®
The *Spirit* of Catholic Living

This book was published by The Word Among Us. Since 1981, The Word Among Us has been answering the call of the Second Vatican Council to help Catholic laypeople encounter Christ in the Scriptures.

The name of our company comes from the prologue to the Gospel of John and reflects the vision and purpose of all of our publications: to be an instrument of the Spirit, whose desire is to manifest Jesus' presence in and to the children of God. In this way, we hope to contribute to the Church's ongoing mission of proclaiming the gospel to the world so that all people would know the love and mercy of our Lord and grow ever more deeply in love with him.

Our monthly devotional magazine, *The Word Among Us*, features meditations on the daily and Sunday Mass readings, and currently reaches more than one million Catholics in North America and another half million Catholics in one hundred countries around the world. Our book division, The Word Among Us Press, publishes numerous books, Bible studies, and pamphlets that help Catholics grow in their faith.

To learn more about who we are and what we publish, log on to our website at www.wau.org. There you will find a variety of Catholic resources that will help you grow in your faith.

Embrace His Word, Listen to God . . .

www.wau.org

Published by The Word Among Us Press
7115 Guilford Road
Frederick, Maryland 21704
www.wau.org

17 16 15 14 13   1 2 3 4 5

ISBN: 978-1-59325-248-9

Cover design by David Crosson

Cover Photo: Catholic News Service

Lumen Fidei
The Light of Faith

ENCYCLICAL LETTER

LUMEN FIDEI

OF THE SUPREME PONTIFF

FRANCIS

TO THE BISHOPS PRIESTS
AND DEACONS CONSECRATED
PERSONS AND THE LAY
FAITHFUL ON FAITH

the WORD
among us®
press